CLASS 90
LOCOMOTIVES

Andrew Cole

AMBERLEY

First published 2018

Amberley Publishing
The Hill, Stroud
Gloucestershire, GL5 4EP

www.amberley-books.com

Copyright © Andrew Cole, 2018

The right of Andrew Cole to be identified as
the Author of this work has been asserted in
accordance with the Copyrights, Designs and
Patents Act 1988.

ISBN 978 1 4456 6696 9 (print)
ISBN 978 1 4456 6697 6 (ebook)

British Library Cataloguing in Publication Data.
A catalogue record for this book is available from
the British Library.

Origination by Amberley Publishing.
Printed in the UK.

Introduction

British Rail identified a need to replace its ageing fleet of AC electric locomotives, and so an order for fifty locomotives was placed with BREL at Crewe. Originally they were to be a development of the successful Crewe-built Class 87 locomotives, and were designated Class 87/2.

It was decided early on in the build programme, however, to reclassify them as a new type in their own right, due to the many differences, both internal and external, and so the class became Class 90.

The first locomotive rolled off the production line in 1987, and was accepted into traffic in 1988. The class was primarily designed to replace the earlier Class 81 and Class 85 locomotives, although the last of these were not withdrawn until the early 1990s.

The class was built for both passenger and freight work, and was equally at home on either. The first twenty-five locomotives were delivered carrying InterCity Swallow livery and were mainly used on passenger work. The next eleven were outshopped in InterCity Mainline livery and were used as general user locomotives, which were available for both passenger and freight services. The final fourteen locomotives were delivered carrying Trainload Speedlink livery and were, in theory, dedicated to freight work.

All fifty locomotives were delivered with ETH equipment and could run at 110 mph, and the freight locomotives could regularly be seen on passenger turns. The freight sector decided to downgrade its locomotives to 75 mph and the ETH equipment was isolated. Those affected were renumbered into the 90/1 series, with the class being split between twenty-four Class 90/0 and twenty-six 90/1 locomotives. Nine locomotives were renumbered for a short while into the 90/2 series, being dedicated to parcels traffic and having composite brake blocks, although they were soon renumbered back.

In the early 1990s, three locomotives were chosen to carry the liveries of the Belgian, German and French state railways, carrying their liveries for around ten years. Five locomotives were transferred to the parcels sector in the early 1990s, and gained RES livery and were dedicated to parcels traffic. The first fifteen locomotives remained on passenger work for their entire lives, working for InterCity on the West Coast before passing to Virgin Trains. They were then sent to Norwich for Anglia passenger turns, working for One Anglia and then National Express East Anglia, and finally Abellio Greater Anglia, replacing the Class 86s, and where they are still in use today.

The class has also been a regular visitor to the East Coast, helping out on GNER and recently Virgin Trains East Coast as well, when the availability of Class 91s has dropped.

Upon privatisation the majority of the class, apart from the first fifteen, passed to EWS or Freightliner, who operate the final ten members of the class. EWS finally became DB Cargo, and they used the class on a variety of workings, having reinstated the ETH equipment and increased the maximum speed back to 110 mph, thus renumbering them back to Class 90/0 locomotives. Freightliner also followed suit, and now the whole class have been renumbered back to their original numbers. The class could, until recently, be found working the overnight Caledonian Sleeper between London and Edinburgh.

Following a downturn in traffic, DB has stored quite a few locomotives at Crewe, some being stripped for spares. No. 90050 suffered fire damage in 2004 and is currently just a stripped shell at Crewe Basford Hall. It will most likely be the first member of the class to be scrapped.

This book takes a look at the lives of this understated class of locomotives, and hopes to tell the story of how they replaced the ageing AC locomotive fleet and revolutionised traffic on BR through privatisation to present day. It includes a shot of every locomotive built, but not every number carried.

No. 90001, 2 January 1992

Class leader No. 90001 *BBC Midlands Today* is seen departing Crewe with a southbound InterCity working. The loco is coupled to the Mark III DVT instead of being coupled to the other end of the stock. This normally occurred when there was a fault with the TDM equipment.

No. 90001, 28 May 1998

No. 90001 works north through Stafford with a rake of Mark III carriages. By this time the loco was working for Virgin Trains West Coast; it would later transfer to Anglia, based at Norwich Crown Point.

No. 90001, 20 April 2002

No. 90001 is seen making a station call at Birmingham International while propelling a Virgin Trains West Coast working through to London Euston. No. 90001 still carries its *BBC Midlands Today* nameplate, and with the impending introduction of the Class 390 units, Class 90 passenger operation on the West Coast had just a couple of years left.

No. 90001, 14 July 2017

No. 90001 is seen stabled at Bescot Yard while en route from Norwich Crown Point to Toton Depot for paintwork issues. The first fifteen Class 90 locomotives passed to Anglia from 2004 onwards to help replace the Class 86 locomotives. No. 90001 now carries the name *Crown Point* in recognition of its home depot.

No. 90002, 8 June 2016

No. 90002 is seen arriving at Ipswich with an Abellio Greater Anglia working to London Liverpool Street from Norwich. No. 90002 carries the name *Eastern Daily Press – Serving Norfolk for 140 Years 1870–2010*. This loco has also carried the names *Girls Brigade* and *Mission: Impossible*.

No. 90002, 17 June 2017

No. 90002 is seen sitting on the buffer stops at London Liverpool Street before heading back to Norwich. This view shows the attractive nameplate off a treat.

No. 90003, 12 October 1988

No. 90003 works south through Adderley Park, in the outskirts of Birmingham city centre, with an InterCity working through to London Euston. At this time the class had not long been introduced, and this was before the Mark III DVTs had been delivered. Unusually, this working has two Mark I brake vans at the front.

No. 90003, 3 September 1994

No. 90003 is seen inside the main repair shed at Glasgow's Springburn Works. This works took over the overhaul of many of the AC electric locomotives from Crewe, who had traditionally repaired the fleet. By this time, No. 90003 carried the name *The Herald*.

No. 90003, 8 February 2003

No. 90003 *The Herald* is seen at Birmingham International while carrying Virgin Trains West Coast livery. This loco, along with the other Class 90s operated by Virgin Trains, would soon pass to Anglia and be transferred to Norwich Crown Point.

No. 90003, 7 September 2004

No. 90003 is seen passing Bethnal Green while propelling a One Anglia service from London Liverpool Street to Norwich. At this time the stock still consisted of Mark II carriages, but they would soon be replaced with ex-Virgin Trains Mark III carriages. No. 90003 carries the name *Raedwald of East Anglia* and One Anglia livery.

No. 90003, 29 June 2015

No. 90003 *Raedwald of East Anglia* passes Bethnal Green while heading for London Liverpool Street. The franchise in East Anglia has gone through a few different operators, as can be seen by No. 90003 carrying National Express East Anglia livery but Abellio Greater Anglia logos as the franchise had changed hands.

No. 90004, 3 March 1990

No. 90004 stands in the sun at London Euston, waiting to depart northbound. This view shows the InterCity Swallow livery which was carried by the first twenty-five locos, and also the small running numbers that were used around this time. This loco would go on to receive the name *City of Glasgow* when it was working for Virgin Trains West Coast.

No. 90004, 29 March 1991

No. 90004 is seen arriving at Birmingham International with an InterCity working from London Euston. The loco had been named *The D'Oyly Carte Opera Company* just one week previously, and still has the silver buffers from its ceremony.

No. 90004, 30 August 1996

No. 90004 *The D'Oyly Carte Opera Company* is seen arriving at Carlisle while heading for Glasgow Central. The Class 90s could be seen the whole length of the West Coast, on both passenger and freight workings.

No. 90004, 5 May 2005

No. 90004 passes Bethnal Green, heading for London Liverpool Street. This loco carries One Anglia livery, which included a rainbow of colours around the cab windows. At this time the franchise had changed hands, and was in fact operated by National Express East Anglia.

No. 90004, 8 June 2016

No. 90004 is seen waiting to depart from Norwich with an Abellio Greater Anglia working to London Liverpool Street. These services operate half hourly, but the Class 90s are due to be replaced by Derby-built electric units. At this time No. 90004 carries the name *City of Chelmsford*.

No. 90005, 7 September 2004

No. 90005 passes through Bethnal Green while heading for London Liverpool Street. This loco carries unbranded Virgin Trains livery and would soon be repainted into One Anglia livery. One was actually operated by National Express, and the fleet was repainted from 2008 onwards into National Express East Anglia livery. This loco was originally named *Financial Times*.

No. 90005, 17 June 2017

No. 90005 *Vice-Admiral Lord Nelson* is seen passing through Shenfield while propelling an Abellio Greater Anglia working through to Norwich. The Class 90s on this route have performed sterling service, but their replacements are on order.

No. 90005, 2 August 2017

No. 90005 is seen at Bethnal Green carrying Abellio Greater Anglia livery. Norwich Crown Point always turn out the Class 90s in excellent external condition, despite the white livery.

No. 90006, 13 June 2013

No. 90006 is seen at London Liverpool Street, having arrived from Norwich. This loco carries the name *Modern Railways Magazine* and former One Anglia livery, but with the logos removed and replaced with Abellio Greater Anglia logos instead. No. 90006 has also carried the name *High Sheriff.*

No. 90007, 3 June 1997

No. 90007 departs Crewe, hauling an InterCity working to London Euston. Crewe was always a good place to see the Class 90 locomotives, with passenger, freight and parcels locos all on view. No. 90007 carries the name *Lord Stamp.*

No. 90007, 8 June 2016

No. 90007, at this time named *Sir John Betjeman*, is seen at Norwich, having just arrived from London Liverpool Street. The passenger Class 90s have all gone through various different names during their career, including No. 90007, which has also carried the names *Keith Harper* and *Lord Stamp*, as in the previous image.

No. 90007, 2 August 2017

No. 90007 *Sir John Betjeman* is seen passing Bethnal Green, heading for London Liverpool Street. The Abellio Greater Anglia livery really suits the class well, and No. 90007 is further enhanced by white-rimmed buffers. The Abellio fleet still retains the buffer rubbing plate and the drophead buckeye coupling.

No. 90008, 21 September 1995

No. 90008 is seen arriving at Manchester Piccadilly with an InterCity West Coast working from London Euston. This loco is seen carrying the name *The Birmingham Royal Ballet*, but today carries the name *The East Anglian*.

No. 90008, 24 May 1998

No. 90008 *The Birmingham Royal Ballet* is seen slowing for the station call at Crewe. By this time these services were operated by Virgin Trains West Coast, with the fleet quickly repainted.

No. 90009, 6 June 1997

No. 90009 is seen at Rugby while heading towards London Euston. This loco carries the name *The Economist,* and of note is the carriage next to the loco, which is one of only three Mark III BFO carriages that, when built, were fitted with a guard's compartment. All three are still in service today with the Great Western Railway. No. 90009 was originally named *Royal Show*.

No. 90009, 29 June 2015

No. 90009 passes Bethnal Green while heading for London Liverpool Street. This loco carries the name *Diamond Jubilee,* and also a large Union Flag on the bodyside, to commemorate Her Majesty the Queen's Diamond Jubilee. The livery carried is former One Anglia, but with Abellio Greater Anglia logos.

No. 90009, 25 November 2016

No. 90009 is seen making a welcome return to the West Coast route, although it was being hauled from Norwich to Crewe for repairs. Major repairs on the Norwich-based fleet are still carried out at Crewe, with the locos being diesel-hauled from East Anglia – in this case by DRS Class 37 No. 37419.

No. 90009, 17 June 2017

No. 90009 is seen approaching Shenfield with an Abellio Greater Anglia working to London Liverpool Street. This particular loco has remained nameless since losing its *Diamond Jubilee* plates.

No. 90010, 15 September 1989

No. 90010 approaches Adderley Park with an InterCity working, heading for Birmingham New Street. This view has changed little in the intervening years, although the line on the right, which passed behind the platform, has been lifted.

No. 90010, 1 May 1993

No. 90010 stands at Edinburgh Waverley, having arrived with a terminating service. By this time the loco had received normal-sized running numbers, replacing the small figures that were applied from new, and it also carries the name *275 Railway Squadron (Volunteers)*.

No. 90010, 17 May 1997

No. 90010 *275 Railway Squadron (Volunteers)* is seen at the other end of the West Coast from the previous photograph, at London Euston. It is seen backing onto a rake of Mark III carriages, having replaced another loco.

No. 90010, 24 March 2009

No. 90010 passes Bethnal Green, heading for London Liverpool Street. This loco carries former One Anglia livery, but has National Express East Anglia logos and would soon be repainted into full National Express livery. This loco was later named *Bressingham Steam & Gardens*.

No. 90010, 17 June 2017

No. 90010 propels an Abellio Greater Anglia working to Norwich from London Liverpool Street through Shenfield. The Abellio fleet works hard on this route, with the service running every half hour throughout the day.

No. 90010, 2 August 2017

No. 90010 heads through Bethnal Green while heading for London Liverpool Street. This is another member of the Abellio fleet that doesn't carry a name, and is one of just four that are in service like this.

No. 90011, 29 March 1991

No. 90011 is seen arriving at Birmingham International with an InterCity working to London Euston. The train consists of a rake of Mark II carriages, including a BSO next to the loco which contains a guard's compartment. No. 90011 carries the name *The Chartered Institute of Transport*.

No. 90011, 20 July 2006

No. 90011 is seen waiting to depart from Norwich with a One Anglia working to London Liverpool Street. At this time the loco carried the attractive One Anglia livery, complete with rainbow colours around the cab windows. No. 90011 has carried various names during its career, including *The Chartered Institute of Transport*, *West Coast Rail 250* and *Let's Go East of England*.

No. 90011, 8 June 2016

No. 90011 *East Anglian Daily Times* arrives at Ipswich with an Abellio Greater Anglia working to London Liverpool Street and a friendly wave from the driver. Of note is the rake of Mark III carriages in use, as they are part of the old Virgin Trains 'Pretendolino' rake that was used by Abellio for a short time to compliment their own carriages.

No. 90012, 30 July 1998

No. 90012 is seen at London Euston carrying full Virgin Trains West Coast livery. This livery was carried by all fifteen members of the VT fleet and was quickly applied following the award of the West Coast franchise. No. 90012 carries the name *British Transport Police*.

No. 90012, 24 March 2009

No. 90012 *Royal Anglian Regiment* passes Bethnal Green, heading for London Liverpool Street. The loco carries former One Anglia livery, but with National Express East Anglia logos applied. Note that the nameplate isn't fitted between the bodyside grills, but is unusually positioned lower on the side.

No. 90012, 8 June 2016

No. 90012 is seen arriving at Ipswich with an Abellio Greater Anglia working from Norwich. This loco still carries its *Royal Anglian Regiment* plates, and they have been positioned in the more traditional place on the loco following its repaint. No. 90012 was originally named *Glasgow 1990 Cultural Capital of Europe*.

No. 90013, 29 August 1989

No. 90013 heads south through Nuneaton with a passenger working to London Euston. The Class 90s were introduced on the West Coast route to help finally eradicate the early AC electric classes – in particular the Class 81s and Class 85s, with the last of those finally being retired in 1991/2.

No. 90013, 13 August 1990

No. 90013 is seen stabled at London Euston along with Class 86 No. 86249. The InterCity Swallow livery sat well on this class of loco. The class was originally to be numbered 87/2, but the locos were redesignated Class 90 before they were released to traffic.

No. 90013, 17 May 1997

No. 90013 *The Law Society* is seen having arrived at London Euston. Despite the loco still carrying InterCity Swallow livery, it had by this time passed to Virgin Trains West Coast and was due for a repaint into Virgin Trains livery.

No. 90013, 8 February 2003

No. 90013 *The Law Society* is seen making a station call at Birmingham International while carrying Virgin Trains West Coast livery. This loco would pass to Anglia within a couple of years, having been replaced on the West Coast by Class 390 units.

No. 90014, 21 May 2000

No. 90014 is seen having arrived at Manchester Piccadilly while carrying Virgin Trains West Coast livery. Of note on this loco is the addition of the flying lady on the cabside, which wasn't carried by all members of the fleet. No. 90014 is another class member to have carried various names, including *The Liverpool Phil*, *The Big Dish* and *Driver Tom Clark OBE*.

No. 90014, 8 June 2016

No. 90014 is seen arriving at Ipswich with an Abellio Greater Anglia working from Norwich to London Liverpool Street. This loco now carries the name *Norfolk and Norwich Festival*.

No. 90015, 26 July 1996

No. 90015 is seen passing southbound through the centre road at Tamworth with an InterCity working to London Euston. This is another example of the loco hauling a train set rather than propelling from the rear. No. 90015 carries the name *BBC North West*.

No. 90015, 17 May 1997

No. 90015 is seen at London Euston, having arrived with a Virgin Trains West Coast working from Wolverhampton. By this time, No. 90015 had lost its *BBC North West* nameplates and had been operated by Virgin Trains for around two months. It would later be named *The International Brigades Spain 1936–1939*.

No. 90015, 6 June 1997

No. 90015 passes northbound through Rugby just three weeks after the previous photograph. In the meantime, it has been repainted into full Virgin Trains West Coast livery. Being one of the earlier repaints, it carries the running number on all four cabsides.

No. 90015, 27 August 1997

No. 90015 arrives at Preston with a Virgin Trains West Coast working from London Euston. The application of the Virgin Trains red livery was certainly a departure from the traditional InterCity Swallow livery.

No. 90015, 13 June 2013

No. 90015 is seen passing Bethnal Green while propelling an Abellio Greater Anglia working towards Norwich. This loco carries the name *Colchester Castle* and full National Express East Anglia livery, but with Abellio Greater Anglia logos.

No. 90016, 14 September 1989

No. 90016 passes through Adderley Park on the outskirts of Birmingham city centre with a rake of Mark II carriages from London Euston. This was one of five Class 90 locomotives that would pass to the parcels sector.

No. 90016, 4 April 1995

No. 90016 is seen at the unusual location of London King's Cross at the head of a parcels working. Five of the class passed to Rail Express Systems for parcels traffic, and all five were repainted accordingly. Note that this loco also retains its rubbing plate and buckeye coupling.

No. 90016, 30 August 1996

No. 90016 rests for the day in the sidings adjacent to Carlisle station. The RES livery suited this class very well, and No. 90016 is seen complete with 'Not to be Moved' board attached.

No. 90016, 29 July 2016

No. 90016 powers south through Nuneaton at the head of a Freightliner Intermodal working. This loco passed to Freightliner when No. 90050 was withdrawn following fire damage, and is seen carrying Freightliner green and yellow livery.

No. 90017, 3 June 1993

No. 90017 is seen departing Doncaster with a mixed bag of parcel-carrying vans. The five RES Class 90 locomotives were the first to be repainted out of their original InterCity Swallow livery, in 1992/3.

No. 90017, 5 October 1995

No. 90017 is seen stabled in the old Motorail loading platform at London Euston. At this time Motorail services had all but ceased, and the loco is seen carrying the name *Rail Express Systems Quality Approved*.

No. 90017, 6 January 2018

No. 90017 presents a sorry sight while in long-term storage at Crewe Electric Depot. This loco has been withdrawn for quite some time and, as can be seen, stripping of spares has started. There are quite a number of Class 90s laid up at Crewe, looking increasingly as if they will never turn a wheel again.

No. 90018, 2 June 1989

No. 90018 works south through Nuneaton while heading for London Euston. The stock includes InterCity as well as blue and grey-liveried Mark II carriages. This shot was taken while No. 90018 still retained InterCity Swallow livery, prior to gaining RES livery.

No. 90018, 29 October 1995

No. 90018 is seen stabled at Polmadie, Glasgow, having now gained RES livery. It is seen among Class 86 locomotives which carry InterCity Swallow and RES livery. No. 90018 would later be named *Pride of Bellshill* when working for DB Cargo.

No. 90019, 6 September 1992

No. 90019 is seen on display at Leicester open day 1992, having not long been repainted into RES livery. It also carries the name *Penny Black*. In the background can be seen No. 90129 carrying pseudo DB German Railways livery.

No. 90019, 1 March 1997

No. 90019 is seen at London Euston, having backed onto the stock of the overnight sleeper from Scotland. The loco would take the stock to Wembley for servicing, ready for the next northbound departure in the evening. By this time No. 90019 had lost its *Penny Black* nameplates, but would regain them before too long.

No. 90019, 20 March 2003

No. 90019 passes light engine through Doncaster, still carrying its RES livery. At the time this loco was on hire to GNER for East Coast passenger workings and was owned by EWS. As can be seen, the loco has been reunited with its *Penny Black* nameplates.

No. 90019, 20 July 2006

No. 90019 *Penny Black* is seen at Norwich while on hire from EWS to National Express East Anglia for passenger work. The former RES examples retained their maximum speed and also their ETH equipment, so they were ideal for passenger work. No. 90019 now carries the name *Multimodal*.

No. 90019, 26 January 2018

No. 90019 *Multimodal* is seen departing from Doncaster while on hire to Virgin Trains East Coast. It is seen propelling a Leeds to London King's Cross working out of the station.

No. 90020, 29 August 1996

No. 90020 is seen at Glasgow Central at the head of a Travelling Post Office working for London Euston. This was the final member of the five to be repainted into RES livery, and it was also named *Colonel Bill Cockburn CBE TD*.

No. 90020, 20 May 2001

No. 90020 is seen at Crewe, being hauled south by classmate No. 90222. No. 90020 was one of the first members of the class to gain EWS maroon livery, and also changed its name to *Sir Michael Heron*.

No. 90020, 20 October 2014

No. 90020 is seen passing through Rugeley Trent Valley on a light engine move heading south. By this time No. 90020 was on its third nameplate, this time being named *Collingwood*, but it still retains its EWS livery.

No. 90021, 29 August 1989

No. 90021 arrives at Nuneaton with an InterCity West Coast working heading north. Nuneaton has changed considerably over the years, but there are still plenty of Class 90 locos to be seen, although all are now on freight workings.

No. 90021, 3 June 1993

No. 90021 is seen arriving at Doncaster, carrying Trainload Speedlink livery, at the head of an InterCity East Coast working consisting of a rake of Mark IV carriages. Nos 90021–24 were operated by Railfreight Distribution at this time, but retained their maximum speed and ETH equipment so they could be used in an emergency on passenger workings.

No. 90021, 26 July 1996

No. 90021 works south through Tamworth with a short automotive working. By this time the loco had received revised Railfreight Distribution livery, which was another livery that really suited the class.

No. 90021, 13 August 2005

No. 90021 is seen working north through Nuneaton while on hire to Virgin Trains West Coast. The loco still retains its revised Railfreight Distribution livery, and this was taken after the end of passenger Class 90 operation on the West Coast, the last service train operated by Virgin Trains using one of their own locomotives being twelve months before.

No. 90021, 15 October 2015

No. 90021 is seen stabled at Bescot. The loco is seen carrying First Scotrail livery but with small EWS logos, as EWS locos were used on the overnight sleeper trains between Scotland and London. There were just three Class 90s painted in this livery, and all have since been repainted.

No. 90022, 12 July 1992

No. 90022 is seen departing Doncaster with a southbound InterCity working and a rake of Mark II carriages. The coaches are mainly first class FK (Corridor First) carriages which formed part of the InterCity charter fleet.

No. 90022, 5 September 1992

No. 90022 is seen on display inside the National Exhibition Centre, Birmingham, as part of the 1992 Freight Connection exhibition, which also included SNCF Class 22 locomotive No. 22317 *La Tour Du Pin*. No. 90022 had been repainted into Trainload Speedlink livery for the occasion, and had also been named *Freight Connection*.

No. 90022, 9 July 1993

No. 90022 *Freight Connection* is seen stabled at London King's Cross while on hire to the InterCity department for use on East Coast workings. The loco was acting as a spare, and the Class 47 alongside, No. 47673 *Galloway Princess*, was in use as a rescue locomotive.

No. 90023, 6 August 1990

No. 90023 is seen at London Euston having been shunt released from its inbound working, which was unusual for the time as most services operated with Mark III DVTs, which eliminated such moves. No. 90023 would go on to be used by the Railfreight sector, losing its InterCity Swallow livery in the process.

No. 90023, 26 June 1993

No. 90023 runs light engine northbound through the centre roads at Doncaster. The loco has now gained Trainload Speedlink livery, complete with Crewe Electric Depot eagle plaque. This loco retained its ETH and maximum speed to allow it to be used on passenger workings.

No. 90023, 31 August 1996

No. 90023 is seen stabled at Heaton Depot, Newcastle, while at the head of a rake of ill-fated Nightstar stock. This stock was to be used on services through the Channel Tunnel to various destinations in the UK but the project was abandoned before it could begin, with the coaches being sold en masse to Via Rail Canada.

No. 90024, 29 March 1991

No. 90024 works south through Birmingham International with a rake of loaded container flat wagons. Despite being in InterCity Swallow livery, this was in fact a freight loco that retained its ETH equipment to be able to work passenger turns – but it still looked odd on a freight working.

No. 90024, 11 August 1997

No. 90024 is seen awaiting departure time at London King's Cross while on hire to GNER for East Coast passenger workings, which would last for a considerable amount of time. It is seen carrying revised Railfreight Distribution livery, but it would later gain unbranded GNER blue livery.

No. 90024, 18 August 1999

No. 90024 stands at Leeds, having just arrived at the head of a GNER East Coast passenger working from London King's Cross. This loco was on long-term hire to GNER to cover Class 91 diagrams and was repainted into unbranded GNER blue livery – the only Class 90 to be so treated.

No. 90024, 3 February 2015

No. 90024 is seen stabled in Wembley yard carrying First ScotRail livery. This loco received this livery to enable it to work overnight sleeper services, and was one of only three members of the class to do so. It is seen alongside classmate No. 90034, which carries Direct Rail Services blue livery.

No. 90024 6 August 2015

No. 90024 works northbound through Lichfield Trent Valley low level in tandem with classmate No. 90035. No. 90024 carries First ScotRail livery. By this time EWS had lost the contract to supply locomotives, and since this shot was taken No. 90024 has been repainted into a special Malcolm advertising livery.

No. 90026, 26 December 1989

No. 90026 spends Christmas 1989 stabled outside Bescot Depot. This loco was the first class member to carry InterCity Mainline livery, which acted as a common user livery for both freight and passenger workings. This livery was only carried by eleven members of the class, Nos 90026–36.

No. 90026, 8 July 2000

No. 90026 is seen stabled at Edinburgh Waverley carrying revised Railfreight Distribution livery. Class 90 locomotives were seen at Edinburgh for many years, both on passenger work and also as traction for the overnight sleeper trains, which is the role No. 90026 is seen performing. This loco carries the name *Crewe International Electric Maintenance Depot* in recognition of the fact that it was home to the Class 92 fleet.

No. 90027, 5 September 1989

No. 90027 is seen departing Birmingham New Street at the head of an InterCity West Coast working to London Euston. This view shows that the InterCity Mainline-liveried locos were just at home on passenger turns as on freight workings.

No. 90027, 27 May 1998

No. 90027 *Allerton T&RS Depot Quality Approved* is seen passing through Crewe station light engine. This loco has now gained Trainload Speedlink livery, but has been renumbered back from No. 90127 following the reinstatement of its ETH equipment and maximum speed.

No. 90028, 3 May 2005

No. 90028 *Hertfordshire Rail Tours* awaits departure time at Birmingham New Street while on hire to Virgin Trains West Coast from EWS. This was after Virgin Trains had ceased using their own Class 90 locomotives. Note that the coaching stock has had its Virgin branding removed.

No. 90028, 24 June 2008

No. 90028 is seen again at Birmingham New Street while on hire to Virgin Trains West Coast. This was following the Grayrigg accident in 2007, which saw Class 390 No. 390033 written off, after which a need arose for a Class 90 and Mark III coaches to be used. The stock retains unbranded Virgin Trains livery, but eventually a rake was repainted into Pendolino livery.

No. 90028, 3 February 2015

No. 90028 stands in the yard at Wembley awaiting its next turn of duty. The loco still retains EWS maroon livery, despite now working for DB Cargo, and some Class 90s have been repainted into DB Cargo red livery.

No. 90029, 5 October 2015

No. 90029 is seen stabled at Bescot carrying DB Schenker red livery. This loco will be remembered as carrying pseudo DB red livery in the mid-1990s as part of the Freight Connection event. This loco once carried the name *The Institution of Civil Engineers*.

No. 90029, 25 October 2017

No. 90029 is seen departing Leeds while on hire to Virgin Trains East Coast. This was during the period that a Class 90 was on hire to VTEC as cover while the Class 91 fleet underwent maintenance. No. 90029 is seen carrying DB Cargo red livery and has had the Schenker part of its logo removed, leaving plain DB logos.

No. 90030, 21 May 2000

No. 90030 stands on display at Crewe Works open day 2000 having just been named *Crewe Locomotive Works*. This plate was previously carried by Class 56 No. 56133 and has since been removed from No. 90030.

No. 90031, 23 July 2000

No. 90031 is seen heading south through Rugby having just been released from overhaul, which included a repaint into EWS maroon livery. This is currently one of the Class 90 locomotives stored long-term and facing an uncertain future at Crewe Electric Depot. This was later named *The Railway Children Partnership: Working for Street Children Worldwide*.

No. 90033, 7 October 1989

No. 90033 is seen at Birmingham New Street, having arrived with an InterCity West Coast working from London Euston. The InterCity Mainline livery suited this class well. At the time, No. 90033 had not long entered service.

No. 90033, 20 January 1991

No. 90033 is seen stabled at Bescot along with classmate No. 90042. The Class 90 freight locomotives would have their ETH equipment isolated and their maximum speed set at 75 mph to keep them on freight turns, and as such they would be renumbered into the 90/1 sub-class.

No. 90033, 6 January 2018

No. 90033 stands forlornly in the yard at Crewe Electric Depot, having been stripped for spare parts. There seems little hope of this loco returning to service as it has donated parts to keep the working members of the DB fleet active. No. 90033 still retains revised Railfreight Distribution livery.

No. 90034, 3 February 2015

No. 90034 is seen stabled at Wembley Yard carrying Direct Rail Services blue livery. Despite the livery this loco was only on hire, instead being operated by DB Schenker at the time. This is the only Class 90 that has carried DRS livery.

No. 90034, 8 June 2016

No. 90034 is seen on the buffer stops at London Liverpool Street. When its hire period finished with DRS, this Class 90 went on hire to Abellio Greater Anglia to help cover a shortage of available passenger locos. No. 90034 is seen carrying plain blue livery, having lost its DRS logos.

No. 90034, 9 June 2017

No. 90034 is seen making a station call at Peterborough, heading for London King's Cross, while on hire to Virgin Trains East Coast. It is carrying unbranded DRS blue livery.

No. 90035, 29 March 1991

No. 90035 is seen at Birmingham International with a rake of Continental Cargowaggons. No. 90035 carries InterCity Mainline livery and is being recessed in Platform Five to allow a passenger working to pass on the main line.

No. 90035, 13 August 2005

No. 90035 powers southbound through Nuneaton with the overnight sleeper train from Edinburgh Waverley to London Euston. Class 90s were the staple motive power on this train for many years. Normally they were EWS-operated locos, but in recent years Freightliner Class 90s have worked the train. Today Class 92 locomotives have replaced the Class 90s.

No. 90035, 11 September 2005

No. 90035 is seen stabled round the back of Crewe station, carrying EWS maroon livery, along with classmate No. 90026. This siding is a favourite place to stable spare locos at Crewe, and is today used to stable the Crewe-based Thunderbird loco.

No. 90035, 9 February 2015

No. 90035 stands on the buffer stops at London Euston, having brought the empty stock from Wembley for the overnight sleeper working to Edinburgh Waverley, where the train will divide. The coaching stock used for the sleeper is due to be replaced with brand-new CAF-built Mark V carriages.

No. 90036, 1 November 2004

No. 90036 is seen at Coventry while on hire to Virgin Trains West Coast. This Class 90 carried a unique livery – a version of the revised Railfreight Distribution livery, but with more yellow applied to the front. No. 90036 now carries DB Cargo red livery and the name *Driver Jack Mills*.

No. 90037, 6 August 1990

No. 90037 is seen running light engine into London Euston, ready to take an InterCity West Coast working north. This was the first Class 90 that was delivered carrying Trainload Speedlink livery, which was carried by the last fourteen members of the class.

No. 90037, 1 December 2015

No. 90037 *Spirit of Dagenham* is seen working south through Lichfield Trent Valley in tandem with classmate No. 90036. No. 90037 carries EWS maroon livery, but has had the logos removed and new DB logos applied.

No. 90038, 21 June 1999

Heading for Leeds while on hire from EWS to GNER, No. 90038 departs from Doncaster. The loco carries revised Railfreight Distribution livery, and can today be found languishing in a sorry state at Crewe Electric Depot, still carrying this livery.

No. 90039, 10 June 1999

No. 90039 is seen passing through Crewe station at the head of a rake of empty flat wagons. The loco carries the livery it was delivered in nearly ten years previously, Trainload Speedlink, despite having been in EWS service for a couple of years.

No. 90039, 21 September 2006

No. 90039 is seen resting at Edinburgh Waverley in between duties on the overnight sleeper train. It is stabled alongside Class 67 No. 67016 and both locos carry EWS maroon livery.

No. 90039, 29 June 2015

No. 90039 is seen stabled at the other end of the West Coast from the previous photograph, London Euston. The loco still carries EWS maroon livery, and over time the running numbers and logos have faded from maroon to white.

No. 90039, 29 July 2016

No. 90039 works southbound through Nuneaton in tandem with classmate No. 90037 *Spirit of Dagenham*. This was a working to Daventry, consisting mainly of Russell and Malcolm containers, which originated in Scotland. Of note is the fact that No. 90039 still carries EWS logos, whereas No. 90037 behind now carries DB logos.

No. 90040, 8 July 2000

No. 90040, which would go on to be named *The Railway Mission*, is seen stabled on one of the through roads at Carlisle station. The loco looks very tired in its Trainload Speedlink livery, but would soon gain a coat of EWS maroon. The railtour in the background was Pathfinder's Skirling Postie tour from Sheffield to Millerhill Yard.

No. 90040, 2 June 2016

No. 90040 passes through Rugeley Trent Valley while working with classmate No. 90029. Both locomotives now carry DB Schenker red livery, but the company would later change its name to DB Cargo.

No. 90040, 15 July 2016

No. 90040 is seen just outside Rugby station, again working in tandem with classmate No. 90029. This time they are seen at the head of a rake of DB-liveried aggregate wagons, heading south.

No. 90040, 15 April 2017

No. 90040 is seen at Bescot Stadium coupled to a rake of first class Mark II carriages. The train was on its way to London to work a Footex the following day, taking Chelsea supporters to Manchester. This is the kind of traffic that the Class 90 locomotives are ideally suited for.

No. 90041, 9 September 2002

No. 90041 is seen at Ipswich carrying Freightliner-branded Trainload grey livery. This loco shows signs of having been renumbered back to No. 90041 from No. 90141. Twenty-six members of the class were renumbered into the 90/1 sub-class when they had their ETH equipment isolated and their maximum speed set at 75 mph. All fifty members of the class later reverted to as-built condition.

No. 90041, 16 July 2013

No. 90041 is seen having passed through Manchester Piccadilly with a rake of empty flat wagons. This had originated from the nearby Trafford Park yard, and No. 90041, by this time, had been repainted into Freightliner green livery.

No. 90041, 31 March 2015

No. 90041 is seen stabled just outside Rugby with a southbound Freightliner working, which had been held up due to engineering work between Rugby and Northampton. Alongside can be seen Class 47 No. 47580, complete with its large Union Flag.

No. 90041, 19 September 2015

No. 90041 is seen stabled at Edinburgh Waverley, waiting to work the overnight sleeper through to London Euston. This loco would spend many months out of traffic, being stored at the Freightliner Midland Road depot in Leeds while awaiting new wheelsets, but has since returned to traffic.

No. 90042, 3 August 1990

No. 90042 is seen making a station call at Birmingham International while on hire to the InterCity sector. This loco was only two months old at the time, and still looks new carrying its Trainload Speedlink livery. Freight locos were a familiar sight on passenger workings at this time.

No. 90042, 20 January 1991

No. 90042 is seen spending the weekend stabled at Bescot. The large black disc to the right of the driver's door is the builder's plate, which was applied by BREL Crewe.

No. 90042, 23 May 2015

No. 90042 works south through Rugeley Trent Valley with Class 66 No. 66416 along for the ride. Both locos carry the new Freightliner Powerhaul livery, which really suits them both well. Applying this livery has been slow, and it is currently only carried by four members of the Class 90 fleet.

No. 90042, 29 May 2015

No. 90042 leans into the curve as it passes northbound through Rugeley Trent Valley, heading towards Crewe. It's been thirty years since the class was first introduced to the West Coast and they are still providing sterling service on AC-hauled freight trains.

No. 90042, 18 September 2015

No. 90042 is seen stabled at Edinburgh Waverley carrying Freightliner Powerhaul livery. Freightliner took over the supply of locos for the overnight sleeper from DB Cargo, but Caledonian Sleeper have now started using their own Class 92s on the services.

No. 90042, 5 September 2017

No. 90042 is seen at Haymarket station with an ECS move consisting of coaches from the overnight sleeper. The Mark III carriages on the sleeper services are now due for replacement with Spanish-built Mark V coaches from CAF.

No. 90043, 18 June 1990

No. 90043, which has only been in traffic for around a month, propels a rake of InterCity-liveried Mark IIIs out of Crewe, heading for London Euston. Eventually the freight sector would restrict the maximum speed on its fleet of Class 90 locomotives, making them harder for the passenger sector to hire.

No. 90043, 9 September 2002

No. 90043 is seen waiting to depart from Norwich with an Anglia Railways service through to London Liverpool Street. By this time the loco had been named *Freightliner Coatbridge* after the company's base in Scotland.

No. 90043, 13 August 2005

No. 90043 *Freightliner Coatbridge* works northbound through Nuneaton at the head of an intermodal working. The Class 57 on the right was employed on Class 390 drags between Nuneaton and Birmingham New Street due to the main line being closed between Rugby and Coventry.

No. 90043, 3 February 2015

No. 90043 stands in the reception sidings at Wembley, having worked up from Ipswich, and will soon head for Crewe. Note that by this time the loco has lost its *Freightliner Coatbridge* nameplates.

No. 90043, 12 March 2015

No. 90043 is seen working through Canonbury on the North London line with an intermodal working from Ipswich towards Wembley. Since this shot was taken, No. 90043 has been repainted into Freightliner Powerhaul livery.

No. 90044, 16 March 2007

No. 90044 is seen passing the signalling centre at Rugby with a southbound Freightliner intermodal working. Amazingly, this loco still carries the original Trainload grey livery it left Crewe Works with back in 1990. It has only received the addition of Freightliner logos, having lost the Speedlink decals it once carried.

No. 90044, 29 January 2013

No. 90044 is seen passing northbound through Nuneaton. By this time the loco has had its Crewe Electric Depot plaque removed from the secondman's cabside.

No. 90044, 21 September 2015

No. 90044 is seen awaiting departure from Rugby with a southbound Freightliner Intermodal working. There are currently just four Class 90s in the Freightliner fleet that still retain this livery.

No. 90045, 18 June 1990

No. 90045 is seen running light engine through Crewe while carrying Trainload Speedlink livery. The loco had been released from Crewe Works just one week previously.

No. 90045, 24 March 1991

No. 90045 is seen stabled at Bescot along with classmate No. 90050. This view shows how the freight locos soon had the drophead buckeye coupling removed. Although they retained the rubbing plates at this time, these have since been removed.

No. 90045, 15 March 2014

No. 90045 is seen in Platform Six at Rugby, waiting for a path south through Northampton while at the head of an intermodal working. The Class 90s work these services through to either Wembley or all the way to Ipswich.

No. 90046, 18 September 2012

No. 90046 is seen powering north through Nuneaton on the Down fast instead of the slow lines. The loco carries Freightliner green livery and is heading for Crewe.

No. 90046, 20 October 2014

No. 90046 works south through Rugeley Trent Valley while hauling Class 66 No. 66591 dead in tow. Both locos carry the original Freightliner green livery.

No. 90047, 13 August 2005

No. 90047 is seen hauling a Freightliner intermodal working south through Nuneaton. This loco has been hauling freights up and down the West Coast for the past thirty years and, with no plans for replacement traction, looks set to continue for the foreseeable future.

No. 90047, 16 September 2015

No. 90047 is seen stabled at Edinburgh Waverley while still carrying its original Trainload grey livery, but with Freightliner logos applied.

No. 90047, 25 March 2016

No. 90047 rests on the buffer stops at London Euston, having arrived with the overnight Caledonian Sleeper service from Edinburgh Waverley. Class 86 No. 86101 *Sir William A Stanier FRS* was attached to the other end to shunt release the Class 90. Note the 'Zero Injuries' sticker adjacent to the cab door.

No. 90048, 6 August 1990

No. 90048 is seen arriving at London Euston at the head of an InterCity West Coast working. This train has a Mark I brake van in place of the more usual Mark III DVT. No. 90048 was only around four weeks old in this view, and still has that new build shine to it.

No. 90048, 16 August 2005

No. 90048 is seen approaching Carlisle with an intermodal working bound for Coatbridge. This view shows off the Crewe Electric Depot eagle plaque nicely; all the Freightliner Class 90s have since had these removed.

No. 90048, 19 June 2015

No. 90048 is seen north of Rugby having just rescued a failed Class 66, No. 66419. The Class 66 had failed in between Northampton and Rugby, causing chaos on one of the main routes south. No. 66419 is operated by Freightliner, but carries unbranded DRS livery.

No. 90048, 8 June 2016

No. 90048 is seen stabled at Ipswich stabling point, still carrying its Trainload grey livery. The scar on the cabside is where the old BR double arrow symbol has been removed. Note that No. 90048 has also lost its Crewe Electric Depot eagle plaque, and the BREL Crewe builder's plate too.

No. 90049, 23 February 2015

No. 90049 is seen approaching Rugby with a southbound intermodal working. The loco carries the new Freightliner Powerhaul livery and was one of just four Class 90s to do so.

No. 90049, 11 May 2017

No. 90049 is seen stabled outside Daventry International Rail Freight Terminal (DIRFT) with classmate No. 90048 for company. The Freightliner Class 90s now work the DIRFT to Coatbridge Russell trains in multiple; DB Cargo Class 90s can also be seen working these heavy trains in tandem.

No. 90050, 24 March 1991

Last-built No. 90050 is seen stabled at Bescot in company with classmate No. 90045. Class 90s were often stabled at Bescot, along with other AC electrics, when working Speedlink services from the yard.

No. 90050, 6 January 2018

No. 90050 stands condemned at Basford Hall Yard, Crewe. This loco suffered fire damage way back in 2004 and has never been repaired, and it looks almost certain that it will be the first Class 90 to be scrapped.

No. 90125, 30 August 1996

No. 90125 is seen approaching Carlisle at the head of an intermodal working. This was the earliest numbered conversion to a Class 90/1, which restricted the locos to 75 mph. This loco was originally delivered carrying InterCity Swallow livery, but has gained Trainload Speedlink livery.

No. 90126, 27 March 1993

No. 90126 *Crewe Electric Depot Quality Approved* is seen inside Crewe Electric Depot having recently been repainted into Trainload Speedlink livery, losing its InterCity Mainline livery in the process.

No. 90128, 15 April 1993

No. 90128 is seen stabled round the back of Crewe station carrying pseudo Belgian State Railways livery. This was one of three Class 90s repainted into European liveries as part of a Freight Connection event, and No. 90128 carries the name *Vrachtverbinding*, the Flemish translation of Freight Connection.

No. 90128, 11 October 1993

No. 90128 *Vrachtverbinding* is seen in the centre of the trio of specially painted European Class 90s at Crewe. All three have been spruced up, with No. 90128 carrying Belgian State Railways livery, No. 90129 German State Railways livery and No. 90130 French Railways livery.

No. 90128, 21 August 1994

No. 90128 is seen on display at Crewe Basford Hall open day 1994. Being painted in pseudo SNCB Belgian Railways livery, this and the other two European-liveried Class 90s were always popular for open day events.

No. 90129, 6 September 1992

No. 90129 *Frachtverbindungen* is seen on display at Leicester open day 1992, carrying pseudo German State Railway livery. This loco, today renumbered No. 90029, now carries DB Cargo livery, which is very similar to this livery.

No. 90129, 20 October 1996

No. 90129 is seen stabled outside Crewe Diesel Depot, awaiting its next turn of service. Looking very similar to the RES parcels-liveried locos behind, No. 90129 carries pseudo German State Railway livery and the name *Frachtverbindungen*.

No. 90129, 3 June 1997

No. 90129 *Frachtverbindungen* is seen passing Stafford light engine while still carrying its pseudo German State Railway livery. The three Class 90s painted in European liveries kept their colours for around ten years before being repainted into EWS maroon.

No. 90130, 27 March 1993

No. 90130, the third of the three European-liveried Class 90s, is seen stabled at Crewe carrying pseudo French Sybic style livery. This livery looked similar to the Trainload grey, but with a deeper top band and orange around the cab windows.

No. 90130, 30 August 1996

No. 90130 *Fretconnection* is seen passing through Carlisle carrying pseudo SNCF French Sybic livery. This livery was based on the French BB 26000 loco livery, and is starting to look a little faded on No. 90130. This was the first of the three European-liveried Class 90 locomotives to lose its special livery.

No. 90131, 27 March 1993

No. 90131 is seen inside Crewe Electric Depot, undergoing maintenance. At this time the loco still retained its InterCity Mainline livery, but it would soon gain a coat of unbranded revised Railfreight Distribution livery and the name *Intercontainer*.

No. 90132, 15 September 1991

No. 90132 is seen on display at Plymouth Laira open day 1991. This is possibly the furthest south a Class 90 has visited, and is a very long way from the overhead wires. No. 90132 still retains InterCity Mainline livery, as does Class 86 No. 86609 alongside.

No. 90132, 28 May 1998

No. 90132 *Cerestar* is seen passing through Stafford with an intermodal working. No. 90132 has by this time been repainted into revised Railfreight Distribution livery, and is today in long-term storage at Crewe Electric Depot.

No. 90133, 27 March 1993

No. 90133 is seen undergoing maintenance inside Crewe Electric Depot, still carrying InterCity Mainline livery. Crewe Electric Depot has been the home for the freight Class 90s for all of their working lives, except for the Freightliner fleet, which is now maintained at the new depot in Basford Hall Yard.

No. 90133, 22 May 1994

No. 90133 is seen on display at Worcester open day 1994. No. 90133 now carries revised Railfreight Distribution livery. The class has proved to be popular visitors to open days over the years.

No. 90135, 3 June 1997

No. 90135 *Crewe Basford Hall* is seen departing from Crewe while hauling Class 92 No. 92031 towards Wembley, and eventually on to Dollands Moor. At this time the Class 92 locomotives had to be hauled from their base in the south, Dollands Moor, to Crewe for repairs and maintenance.

No. 90136, 6 June 1997

No. 90136 is seen approaching Rugby carrying its experimental Railfreight Distribution livery. The loco is employed on hauling Class 92 locos Nos 92026 *Britten* and 92042 *Honegger* north to Crewe for repairs. Today No. 92042 is in service with DB Cargo; meanwhile, No. 92026 has been exported to Bulgaria.

No. 90138, 21 September 1995

No. 90138 runs light engine through Manchester Piccadilly, having dropped off its intermodal working at the nearby Trafford Park. This view clearly shows the lack of drophead buckeye coupling and also the removed rubbing plate between the buffers.

No. 90140, 15 October 1994

No. 90140 is seen stabled round the back of Crewe station along with classmate No. 90138. Both locos carry as-built Trainload Speedlink livery. The whole fleet of fifty locomotives eventually had their ETH equipment reinstated and their maximum speed set to 110 mph, and are now all numbered as Class 90/0.

No. 90142, 23 April 1996

No. 90142 is seen running light engine into Manchester Piccadilly while heading for Trafford Park to pick up its intermodal working, which it will later take south. By this time No. 90142 is starting to look a little scruffy and faded, and yet it only had six years of service behind it.

No. 90142, 3 June 1997

No. 90142 is seen racing north through Stafford with a Freightliner intermodal working. By this time No. 90142 has lost its Speedlink decals and just carries unbranded Trainload grey livery.

No. 90142, 22 May 2000

No. 90142 is seen at London Euston while on hire to Virgin Trains West Coast. Despite the fact that the railway was privatised over three years previously, No. 90142 still carries its British Rail double arrow on the far cabside. This was an unusual choice for hiring, as being numbered No. 90142 meant that it was limited to 75 mph.

No. 90144, 10 June 1999

No. 90144 is seen speeding south through Warrington Bank Quay while at the head of a Freightliner intermodal service. This view is unmistakable with the large Lever factory in the background.

No. 90145, 21 August 1994

No. 90145 is seen on display at Crewe Basford Hall open day 1994. This yard always produced an excellent open day, having such a large area in which to display the locomotives. No. 90145 shows signs of having been renumbered from No. 90045 on the cab front.

No. 90145, 28 May 1998

No. 90145 works a rake of empty Freightliner flat wagons northbound through Stafford, heading for Crewe, while carrying Freightliner logos on top of the old Trainload grey livery. Today this loco has been repainted into Freightliner Powerhaul livery and carries the number 90045.

No. 90146, 23 April 1996

No. 90146 rounds the curve into Manchester Piccadilly with a loaded Freightliner intermodal working for Trafford Park. At the time of this photograph the Cross-Country services that visited Manchester were still loco hauled, as can be seen with the Class 86 in the background.

No. 90146, 16 June 2000

No. 90146 is seen departing Carlisle on the back of a Virgin Trains West Coast working to London Euston. This was a regular loco on hire, along with No. 90142, and they appeared numbered as both 90/0 and 90/1 while on hire. Again this seems a strange move, since they were limited to 75 mph as Class 90/1s.

No. 90148, 21 May 2000

No. 90148 is seen stabled at Crewe Basford Hall Yard. This was on the occasion of the nearby Crewe Works open day, and the yard at Basford Hall was also available to view, which was a nice touch as there were no moves planned in the yard on that day.

No. 90149, 30 August 1996

No. 90149 is seen bringing a lengthy Freightliner intermodal working towards Carlisle. It is heading for the lines that avoid the platforms, and will probably have a crew change while at Carlisle. Today, No. 90149 carries the latest Freightliner Powerhaul livery, having been renumbered back to No. 90049.

No. 90150, 6 June 1997

Last-built No. 90150 is seen approaching Rugby with a northbound intermodal working. Rugby has seen significant changes since this shot was taken, with new platforms being added and other lines lifted, including the adjacent one with the buffer stops.

No. 90150, 28 May 1998

No. 90150 is seen heading north on the slow lines through Stafford. This loco was taken out of service following fire damage that it received in 2004 and its future looks perilous, having been heavily stripped of parts at Crewe.

No. 90222, 20 May 2001

No. 90222 *Freight Connection* is seen hauling classmate No. 90020 *Sir Michael Heron* through Crewe while carrying revised Railfreight Distribution livery. In 2001 nine members of the fleet were renumbered into the 90/2 sub-class after they received brake modifications and composite brake blocks to work high-speed parcels traffic. No. 90222 is today in long-term storage at Crewe Electric Depot, having been renumbered back to No. 90022.

No. 90225, 20 May 2001

No. 90225 is seen stabled outside Crewe Diesel Depot while carrying Trainload Speedlink livery. The nine members of the 90/2 sub-class were renumbered for just over twelve months before being renumbered back into the main series.